Perfume and Opium

by
Leon Gratton

Grosvenor House
Publishing Limited

All rights reserved
Copyright © Leon Gratton, 2020

The right of Leon Gratton to be identified as the author of this
work has been asserted in accordance with Section 78
of the Copyright, Designs and Patents Act 1988

The book cover is copyright to Leon Gratton
Front cover image: credit needed to www.123rf.com/profile_velveteye

This book is published by
Grosvenor House Publishing Ltd
Link House
140 The Broadway, Tolworth, Surrey, KT6 7HT.
www.grosvenorhousepublishing.co.uk

This book is sold subject to the conditions that it shall not, by way of
trade or otherwise, be lent, resold, hired out or otherwise circulated
without the author's or publisher's prior consent in any form of binding or
cover other than that in which it is published and
without a similar condition including this condition being imposed
on the subsequent purchaser.

This book is a work of fiction. Any resemblance to
people or events, past or present, is purely coincidental.

A CIP record for this book
is available from the British Library

ISBN 978-1-78623-662-3

CONTENTS

PERFUME AND OPIUM	1
BROKEN MOON	3
SILVER AND GOLD	4
FLICKERING STARE	5
FLOWERS	6
TRUE ANGELS	7
THE GUILDS	8
DARK	9
A LITTLE BIT OF EVERYTHING	10
SERPENT STINGS	11
DIRT	12
HAIKU #1	12
SILENT SILENCE	13
SOUL FOOD	14
CHILDREN OF THE RAIN	15
DANCE THROUGH FIRE	16
SMOKE ON IN THE BLUES (SONG)	18
MYSTIQUE	20
WORLD SO CRUEL (SONG)	21
TWIST	23

GRACE	24
TOUCH	25
MOON AND STARS	26
COMFORT SMOKE (SONG)	27
WOMAN SO DARK	29
THE SLAVE AND THE NYMPH	30
ACID BLUES (SONG)	31
POETIC INTERLUDE	33
MOOMBE	34
SKIES	35
BULLETS	36
WINTERTIME RAIN	37
PEEL	38
ADDICTIVE ADDICTS	39
SOLDIERS ADDICTION	40
KISS	41
TWIST pt1	42
WISE ANGEL	43
CRYSTAL TEAR	44
DISCREET	45
REAPERS GAME	46
NO HEART	47
EXOTIC	48
HOURGLASS	50
EARTH BOUND SLAVE	51
LIZARD MAN COMETH (SONG)	53
UGLY TO ANGRY	55

LOVE IS AN ANGEL	56
DYING RAIN	57
EARTH SHAKER	58
BLUE TEAR (SONG)	59
SOCIETY A TOMB	61
UNFOLD YOUR WINGS	62
SAVE	63
UNKNOWN PLACE	64
OLD BLUE (SONG)	65
EYES	66
GODS	67
EVER AND NEVER	68
RINGS ON FINGERS (SONG)	69
MYSTIC	71
AZURE BONDS	73
TRUE	74
ROSE OF LOVE	75
LIES	76
DANCE ON	77
WOMAN SO DARK	78
BITTER	79
MIDNIGHT BLUES (SONG)	81
SUN	83
TOMBS OF RUST	84
FORGOTTEN SUNS	86
TOY	87

PERFUME AND OPIUM

The quiet time
All a sundry
Shall turn your mind
And make you wonder
With passions pen
And feeling of thunder
The movement Zen
Is it just dreams?
I wonder
They come in colour
No longer black and white
Dawn takes my mind and changes it
Even tho' I'm in over my head
You know that girl
I dream of each day
Some people move
To sullen quiet ways
Silent to whisper
My heart on the mend
Quiet yet crisper
I need another friend
Don't attract the trouble
As colour and light blend
My time of words
The night is drawing in

I'll wait till tomorrow
(Enclose me in your gentle rain)
Those acid words of beauty
Shall go again
I miss the cruelty
Of a night in someone's head
With Lords and Deities
I'm glad she never said
Oh karmic beauty
I am a fledgling
To be fed
And times of security
She drowns my sorrow in her head
I smell perfume and opium
In this world, like I said
The need for security
Is gone and quietly fed

BROKEN MOON

My opening eyes
Set to starlit skies
The moon quietly broken
Sad yet happy
Torn and scrappy
I want a life
Purity a wife
The angels give us reason
Without time flowing out of season
The niceties of eyes
The misty velvet skies
Stars becoming condemned
But ancients give us time to mend
Quietly dawn comes
And night slips away
Do you need summer to wander
As life to the foolish is squandered
Read, write express yourself
Many a night I've thought about the earth

SILVER AND GOLD

The sound of the soul
Reaching out to get nearer its goals
The quiet word with finger signs
Shall show re-birth in the skies
The fortune of water
The stories untold
Of princess's going to pentacles of gold
My thoughts flowing
Whilst the moon unfolds
The Quietness coming to lives of the bold
Heroes ride their Pegasus's
Whilst dragons become mist
I gave her the moon
You know it exists
Delphi now raven with silver and gold
Whilst I turn Elven to kill and change the
Spiders soul

FLICKERING STARE

Sweet as honey
The scented air
With quiet times running
Strawberry fair
My soul gone quietly
To the promise of a flickering stare
The souls Soliquity
Quietly we share
Some feel lust
Then put to shame
Others its trust
And never a game

FLOWERS

My world turned upside down
Moving fast away from the wrong side of town
Whilst animals bear down, on my flesh
The world is silent with humour
The world is treasure
Women to a poet, all eyes treasure
But some
Oh so winsome
A beauty you can't measure
I've been caught in their wickedness
And torn by their thunder
But to me forgiven
As they have innumerable pleasures
Some it's eyes
Some it's smiles
Others its bodies, all the while
Quiet I wait, wander and watch
The flowers all breaking
Yes I want to touch

TRUE ANGELS

People moved me to thought
With weakness's all gone
The sunlight shone on the throne
And I wonder what I'm doing
In this world, when love is so cruel
No one woman will be mine
They want to set me up with sharpened knives
So I fall onto sensuality
With true Angels

THE GUILDS

Midnight vigil in the church of the sinners rest
The guilds all open to the sins of the blessed
With an unknown quantity the world goes by
A universal explosion in the blink of an eye
Wicked resentful all say goodbye
People turning on their neighbours for bloody revenge
The end will never happen because we're quietly strange!

DARK

Fact is fiction
So where is truth?
Lies are poison
So where is proof
End in the middle
So where is the start?
Believe in the forgiven
Even after dark!

A LITTLE BIT OF EVERYTHING

A little bit of everything
Which is what you are to me
A quiet bit of something
To be there and to be seen
A wonder of melodies
Yes you sing so sweet
A loving girl of wonderment
With soul fill glances and eyes
As deep as the sea

SERPENT STINGS

The serpent stings
Whilst we hiss and spit
Rumours get worse
Whilst the weak have to survive
With time on the war path
The cornered man takes the punches
Dogs of war go on running
Whilst the politician takes brunches
Aren't we all smiling?
In this world of tower houses
And whores take of everything
Except their bosom blouses

DIRT

You go chasing waterfalls
And ended up with a handful of dirt

HAIKU #1

Small things lead to
Larger thoughts

SILENT SILENCE

The silent silence
With no going back
I lose time on track
With a dark drip of honey
Who feels for me
I look out into this valley
And smile, dilly dally
She is a wonder and hope is blooming
This quiet musical way
More gorgeous you've become
Stroke my face
With magical trace
Your heart going on a summer's day
Your eyes your soul I long to explore
Yes Dawn of day it's you I adore

SOUL FOOD

The space I give
Whilst life you live
I'm a sorrowful heart
Please remember the start
Quiet I wait
Wondering whether you'll love me soon
It's granted your words
In the hope of love
Traced in my eyes are heavens above
But no one believes in poetic slaves
They think it's set to graves
With music reflecting our very mood
Love in the kitchen set to soul food

CHILDREN OF THE RAIN

True I've come to this place over and over
And over again
Where silence sleeps in time and in
Pain
Promise I will love you without the
Grayness and insane
Tho' love will show you why we
Are children of the rain?
The blue skies continue to be shallow
In there way
And somehow I miss you on a
Fateful day

DANCE THROUGH FIRE

Dance through fire
Dance through shadows
It's the only way to come through the
Rain
Dance through Ice
Dance through Dust
Then time will tell you who you can
Trust
Dance through rain
Dance to heavens
Where we will be together
Forever
Dance under the moon
Dance to fallen stars
Then you will see love eases the
Ugliest of scars
Dance on warriors
Dance on Lovers
But both should remember they are
Sisters and brothers
Dance with love
Dance with souls
Make sure you are going to
The pearly gates
Dance through Fire

Dance through shadows
Soul filled eyes, time with the small
Voice, taken with purity, taken by choice
Left with a decision, left in the firelight
Shadow of indecision

SMOKE ON IN THE BLUES (SONG)

It's coming with light
The openness the night
My heart open on the mend
The girl gone
The place the smoke

Shadows with stars
People moving in the toughest bars
Never saw women with such stone
The girl gone
The place in smoke

It's quiet in this room
The girl broke my heart real soon
So smoke on in the blues
So smoke on in the blues

With time drawing in
The devil dreamed of original sin
Fire blew me your way
The girl gone
The dance to smoke

Quiet my world with angel's tears
People live quiet in this tomb of fears
The women go on their way
The girl gone
The chance to smoke

It's quiet in this room
The girl broke my heart too soon
So smoke on in the blues
So smoke on in the blues
So smoke on in the blues
So smoke on in the blues

MYSTIQUE

Mystique
With a bleak
Solemn sneak
It could keep
But we all seek
That unknown hypnotic peek
The soldiers sleep
Knowing that wives weep
At the times golden tick
Never mind the tock
It buzzes with a clock
They tumble when we get a shock
And rumble at peoples thoughts

WORLD SO CRUEL (SONG)

The world of people cold
The blues all rhyming in my head
People all dancing to the dead
With a world slowly bled
Everywhere gone to a world so cruel

Take it down turn it round
To a world so cruel
The open blade the duel

Well here it comes again
Don't really care what he said
I've been through the valley of the dead
With time of blues spilling out my head
I've seen the holy in the sunlight

Take it down turn it round
To a world of bright light
The open night the fight

Well they say don't give up your day job
But this is a perfect way to express myself
And bough to gold
I'm set to hells evil soul
The people all cry but I'm going to win

With a world so cruel
Pick me up baby ooo so cool
Try life in delight
Try life in delight
Try life in delight

TWIST

To wait and hold for a twist of fate
To wean yourself of narcotic bliss
To assume power in the silvery mist
Love lays down
Love grows large
Love turns and twists
Magical mechanical with power
Of the sun
Heaven fits freely into the palms of some
Faces so glad to know that
Life is not it all
Love lays down
Love grows large
Love turns and twists

GRACE

Grace of my heart
With the sun we fight the dark
Face the way of this race
So we don't vanish without a trace
The evil has ended
It's in its place
The fire of spirit
Has tamed the wicked ways
The power of will
Conquering all
A disgrace in heaven
Led to their fall
But love in our hearts
Will unite us all

TOUCH

His face sublime, beautiful in all
Times and all minds
Precious and petty the brothers war on
Misbelieve and retrieve the count is six
To hope he'll change and turn
A place evil and strange
Into one of joy and hope
We're all in place to save the human race!
With not so much as a little trace
Of hate, envy, regret or such
This world has been to long out of
Touch
The days are counting
The end is near
End of what is all I hear!

MOON AND STARS

Tree of life
For your wife
Piercing of flesh
But not by a knife
Needles of paint
To mark my time
Neither shall shudder
Neither shall scar
Moon and stars

COMFORT SMOKE (SONG)

Electric woman with looks of passion
You are truly wondrous and in fashion
The believers, the mysterious
People see us and don't know
Your world, take it real slow

You are a dream
Yes I can see you on the scene
Comfort smoke!
Glad your honey!
See you almost spoke!

I want your eyes your soul
My heart set to your sun
But you changed your mind so suddenly
Leaving me with tears
Caution like playing with fate

You are a dream
Yes I can see you on the scene
Comfort smoke!
Glad your honey!
See you almost spoke!

Comfort smoke!
Comfort smoke!
Comfort smoke!
Comfort smoke!
See you almost spoke!

WOMAN SO DARK

The opening heart becomes so sweet
The feeling so strange we move to the
Beat
Sugar and spice
That feeling so nice
Yet not very old
The hold so stark
And turning cold!
This feeling of love
Growing slightly old
And appearing from above

THE SLAVE AND THE NYMPH

Suspicion arrived
On a cloudy day
Of a town of jealousies
And triangular ways
Peace came from heaven
Performed in ink
Only to be taken
By a darkened nymph!
Love then bound
The sunlight and rays
The Nymphs stolen poems
Were given back to the slave
And the Nymphs darkened jealousy
Of the talented slave
Were lain on a pillow
Of sunlight and rays
Fear struck the Dragon
Whose curse on the Nymph
He had seen this coming
When he had sent the Nymph
Now the slave and the Nymph
Bound by love
Have slain the evil dragon
With three heartfelt words!

ACID BLUES (SONG)

Love in romance
Take that chance
Hold me in your arms

It's a pulling way
With us being love filled slaves
The true eyes of beauty
Don't hold our love in regret

Love in romance
Take that chance
Hold me in your arms

Dawn I'm looking your way
And finality has beautiful ways
You are truly caught in a summer shower
Dance with me in the shadow of the
Tower

Love in romance
Take that chance
Hold me in your arms

Gone to godlike ways
It's in poetic charms

My redemption in a lover's soul
The acid blues show us unknown

Love in romance
Take that chance
Hold me in your arms
Show me lover's charms
The very light you have shown
Whilst this feeling comes home
Love in romance

Take that chance
Hold me in your arms
Help me through this storm!
ACID BLUES (SONG)

OH DAWN!!
OH DAWN!!

POETIC INTERLUDE

Dawn of day, in the unknown ways
Will become resolute in the winters rays
With time we shall steal warm singing sayings
And with this become holy ones whilst
They think on love filled plays
The life you led was in the head
Of a man and poppy slaves
You turn your back and say okay
But loving you is the only way

MOOMBE

Piece of apple for time to last
Hoping she comes
To seal my past
Angelical floating on air and gasps
A petrified hair
To make me laugh
She smiled as the nuts
Went in the bin
Her wings fluttering
Our love will win
She kisses me gently and
Shows me a spell
Not cold or dark
But heavenly and tell
MOOMBE!!!

SKIES

Great wonder of love and life
I hope with grace we'll meet in time
And even friendship springs to mind
Sullen confusion love will open eyes
Coldness comes in the waning moon
But silence leaves its own wounds
Spell like wish I apologise
I neither want hers or my demise
I'll smile when I see you
And trade your eyes
To one look
To one smile
To one thought
I give you the SKIES!!

BULLETS

*THIS POEM IS TO MY COUSIN
WHO FOUGHT IN BOSNIA
TO DANNY YOU'VE BEEN
THROUGH ENOUGH*

With marching men
Where is the compassion
They go to fight battles
And save lives
Studded bullets
Sharpened knives
They lay down their honour
And leave behind wives
Become so sudden, too the rape
The graves
And the reasons of battle, opium
Land or to hold religion as slaves
But the people are crying
Whilst the soldier sits in silence
Never knowing if its reason to
Violence

WINTERTIME RAIN

Wintertime rain
Cold and freezing
Shows us the world is truly bleeding
Glad we are in glowing houses
Where love and fashion shows us warmth
Night crawls in
And day gently away
When women dress warm
And love comes and stays
Quietly I think of wintertime rain
Where comfort and passion
Steal us away

PEEL

The moon in its way
Sends me forth on the seas lapping sway
The love I feel is blind and turned
My heart melted I could easily PEEL!
With Valium or Benzedrine so that I no longer feel
The drugs I do are unreal
In the fact that I no longer beg, borrow or steal
I'm in habitual thoughts
Bringing forth psychosis that I haven't
Been taught
My world blood, wounds since childhood
Am I always going to be the addict?
With a doctors way and a script
These poisons that I've sipped
Alone I'd be as well cooking up a
Bone
And leaving the world forever
But then I look at Dawn and see
The night gently fades
Hell I destroyed a ring of nightshade
As much as I believe
There are other ways to receive
Love, tenderness and prayer
The many mused musings

ADDICTIVE ADDICTS

It's cold out there
She stands there bare
My heart with gladness
Takes it away
The mist forming watching for the stare
I will quit the habit
I will quit the pills
The thing has a hold
And life nothing but bold
Addictive addicts
Yes I'm an ex junkie
I recognise the problem

SOLDIERS ADDICTION

Got two races going to war
With guns and bombs and two swords
The fork of the devil reaches to us
Skewering lives with lust
Leaving a garden of stone
For us to live in
No one loses
But no one wins
Left to decay the soldier's addiction
Left with a paranoid affliction

KISS

Traced on my face is pain
And suffering
With hell in my head I'm only
Bluffing
With shadows I have spoken
Lace and diamonds I set
Foot on the wrong path
Whilst I take this unholy
Bath
I plunge deeper into this
Abyss
I know now I should have
Stolen that KISS!

TWIST pt1

Sane so sane I only feel pain
Rain down the drain
Enough to drive you insane
Brains to be tamed
The dark side is a game
Love sweet Love
Is it only when you're in touch?
Love deathly Love
Like a deadly kiss
Take to the skies with the
Crawling fly
Dark is its kiss
Hard as stone is its fist
Patience is true
Patience is bliss
For not all succumb to its
TWIST!!!!

WISE ANGEL

A Tear rolled out of my eyes
Tearing through my disguise
For the wisest angel to see
My pain my suffering
My very soul
Soon she would show me
How to put my Love on
Hold!!

CRYSTAL TEAR

We live in sad times
We live with broken minds
We sometimes miss the signs
We stumble around as if we're blind
The dragon unfolds its heart
The princess wakes with a start
Love unfolds from her mind
The dragon moves as if he's blind
Following only the beating of her
Heart!
Then he finds
A blue crystal tear
And he no longer cowers in fear
For the dragons heart lays still
And as he dies
She sheds her disguise
And they both fly on to the purple
SKIES!!!!

DISCREET

Summers coming a golden
Warm sun
People go out to meet
Other people on the street
Children play
Lovers hold hands and
The bustle of the city
Carries on
The traffic rumbles and
Faces become pure
Daylight rambles on
Mystical tours looking for
Things that come in dreams
And loving places to
Be discreet

REAPERS GAME

My world is slowly coming
Apart
Maybe it's true I don't have
A heart
But to love so much under
This moon
Heavenly creatures don't
Care if I live or die
So once again I speak to
The dragon's eye
Mystical words
Mystical signs
She knows I love her
But she won't be mine
A battle of words
A battle of plays
If she comes I'll love her
More each day
I'll ease her pressure
I'll show her treasures
That no world could count
Psyche, Delphi Dawn or
Whatever her name, life is
To mysterious to play
The reapers GAME!!!!

NO HEART

The arrows
The hourglass
The stars
Fair
The gold
The ring
The vows
Fair
The people
The lust
The dagger
But no heart

EXOTIC

The movie plays and I
Know what the future
Holds dark and fantastical
A dreary hell

People talk of reason
Rhyme and self
Doubtful and yet graceful
The old gods live with
Ourselves

It's not just puzzles
Which the Master teaches
It's beauty in wonder
Which the Buddha preaches

Mostly creatures of the new
Moon become well being
Wonder and loving I think
Of the earth's healing ways

The people move on to the
Bustle of the street and
Finally Dawn comes and I
Feel her touch warm and
Gentle with such and
Such
The taste EXOTIC!!!

HOURGLASS

The bonds of the sea
Rise and fall
With waves of many
And lives so small
The blue waves which
Lightning fell
Leaves us to wonder
If it's the gates to Hell

Time on pebble with Sand
And Brass
The moon its controller
With hourglass

EARTH BOUND SLAVE

I had a lover once
She cared for me
She set me free
Now all I've got
Is a broken heart
With little care

I had passion once
For this world
For a handful of girls
With a head full of curls
Since I let the diamond go
The pain is slow

Now I don't want to be
Passions slave
Or crouching at my grave
With tears in my eyes

Trying to forget the past
With Lovers who never last
And feelings which drive most
INSANE!!
Turning quiet
Turning away

I watch as lovers go by
Shedding both tears and light
From my eyes
It's my heart that spoke
Of dragons fire
And unearthly desire

The golden sun
Which produced
The shadows grave
Shall be the one
Of earth bound slave

LIZARD MAN COMETH (SONG)

True enough it's been tough
With some psycho sexual
Insect sucking my blood
Peace on earth I hope so
Cause I don't take a blow
Like that for no reason
No, no, no, no

Crime spree cannabis free
Where would be the fun
To take something pleasurable
And let it run
Brains a mess, haven't even
Got someone to bless
No, no, no, no

Love beads half undressed
But if she doesn't move
She'll miss the rest daggers
Of flesh summoned by eyes
We need to see into starlight
Skies

LIZARD MAN COMETH!!
No, no, no, no
LIZARD MAN COMETH!!
No, no, no, no
LIZARD MAN COMETH!!
No, no, no, no
He havin' too much fun
He havin' too much fun
He havin' too much fun
He havin' too much fun

UGLY TO ANGRY

True life is bleak
For the ones who seek
An answer to life's mysteries
Mother Nature is hard to please
And our holy father holds all
The keys
And the blessing way is
Hidden in the trees
Places so bleak
Faces of the meek
Change from ugly to angry

LOVE IS AN ANGEL

To die a death a million times
To ride what's left on wind filled
Rhymes
To see the best fall to their knees
To run from hell and heaven to seize
With words I spoke a million times
With heart of gold I write these rhymes
With promises I broke the unseen lines
She moves with the grace of an angel
She challenges the way of the devil
She spoke the words into her pillow
Her eyes began to weep just like the
Willow
The tree woke in time for spring
And with a heavenly voice it began
To sing
A dragonfly flew around its bark
And light up the heavens with a spark

DYING RAIN

To walk in streets of purest gold
To walk in streets of coldest cold
To walk in streets where I sold my
Soul
To take your love and put my
Life on hold
To see Jack Frosts eyes tinkle
To see the ice from his fingers
Sprinkle
To see the evil in the bumper of
A car
To watch the heavens under a
Star
To make the poor humble again
To make them ease the stinging Pain
To make them see life is far from
Sane
To watch them in the windows of
The dying rain

EARTH SHAKER

Sorrow strikes at my shattered
Heart
A child who screamed at the
Dark
A dog's bite is worse than it's
Bark
But still I love you with all
My Heart
You look and talk like a
Star maker
I look and see you are a
Dream waker
And also an earth shaker
Love comes
Love goes
But your eyes, your soul
Have put my love on hold

BLUE TEAR (SONG)

Ceremonies come and go
But your eyes have put
My love on hold

Your very soul is with
Me
Your love has bit me

Now I am far gone away

The tears I cry are blue
And clear

I wish I didn't live in fear
Of what could be

I'm trying not to let you
Wake

I'm praying nearly every
Day

I'm wanting you to be
Right here

I'm in the dragons bright
Blue tear
I'm in the dragons bright
Blue tear

SOCIETY A TOMB

Society is a tomb
And narcotics its womb
With raving, craving addicts of lust
It's as simple as forgetting trust
No one likes the cold numb weather
And angels weigh their hearts against
A feather
Girls and women all beautiful on this
Earth
Whilst man serves up evil at what
It's worth
Rings on fingers
Are what they seem
Rings on fingers
Mean the earth to me
Couples hold hands
And the world turns with sands
Dawn with her radiance
Rings on fingers
But they somehow seem false

UNFOLD YOUR WINGS

The cold day with a blond here
She was dressed pretty with a pink
Scarf
Her body a tease
Her eyes set me at ease
A party girl, I bet she is
I'm still living in the dawn of hope
I wonder if I'll see her again
But Dawn, I don't fall in love every day
And if you are a golden princess
Let it shine
I love you and you are divine
I hope we never cross words again
The gentle mind, the gentle rain
With days of hope and days of pain
Your raven hair
Your golden stare
So she is blond
But never in your shadow or your
Beauty
Angelic you look
Unfold your wings
Enclose me as gentle you sing

SAVE

Sweet sorrow as our souls
Collide
People and places seem so
Fine
When our sweet souls
Collide
My life has but one meaning
That is to meet your soul
In the heavenly sky
We show compassion to
The weak
Then we turn and swear
"We hate, we are meek"
Our love shines through
All this jealousy and
Rage
And that is why my love
I save, for you

UNKNOWN PLACE

A veil of satin covers my body and
Face
It set my love filled heart at
Another pace
And leaves my soul with a
Trace
Of love, and serenity for the
Human Race
She whispers so quietly from that
Unknown place
And then my heart begins to
Race

OLD BLUE (SONG)

I had a dream
That you were with me
Your arms around me
Showing me love
You loved me tender
You loved me true
Loved me until my heart
Turned blue

Now I'm just a lonely soul
Whose lost control
Of what I do
I'm just a vagabond
In this town
Of cocaine gas and glue
OLD BLUE
OLD BLUE
I'm just a vagabond
In this town
Of cocaine gas and glue
OLD BLUE
OLD BLUE

EYES

Beauty are in these eyes
Which alight to the heavenly
Skies
My breath taken momentarily
Leaves me to sigh
A beam of light from the
Morning dawn
Touches my heart and I sing a
Song
Floating on the highness of
Life
Hope she will become wife
This creature called
Life
But then we must part
One day and I must ride
That beam of light

GODS

They take human disguise
They flitter before your eyes
They act and seem so shy
But it is all a white lie
GODS SING
GODS ACT
Gods will break the satanic
Pact

EVER AND NEVER

Life's blood slowly flowing
Life's love brightly glowing
The worlds end is now showing
Rain so cold
Pain so bold
The future so bleak
The rich feed off of the weak
Our destinies we all shall seek
Ever and never sin we speak

RINGS ON FINGERS (SONG)

I was waiting forever
The pleasure never given
I feel nothing with very little
The love I want was just returned

The grace of my heart was
Too much for you
The pace of my mind is so
Slow it would leave you blind

You say thinking thoughts
Of utter Love
I've seen poor desperate
People pray for a dove

Peaceful watching waiting
For the sun
It's just around the corner
We are all chosen ones

Now you say blood red moon
Solar wicked flares
I miss you so much it drives
Me to despair

The grace of my heart
Was too much for you
The pace of my love is so
Slow it would leave you blind

The delta blues of true love
Would show you
That I'm always true
RINGS ON FINGERS!!!!
RINGS ON FINGERS!!!!
RINGS ON FINGERS!!!!

MYSTIC

"MYSTIC!" he cried
"A fool to some"
"Time to leave"
The voice of the champion spoke
Softly, showing the power of
The spear and yolk
"Eggs my lady! Eggs"
She rose quietly and crossed
Her legs
The fool. The Mystic
But never the thief
Beyond Imagination
Beyond belief
Incarnation
Goat's milk bathed
Trying to make me into
An overplayed sage
Headache! She screamed
Headache, Headache,
Close the web
A voice seemed to say
Weapons are valueless
Cause we're unafraid
"Devil incarnation"
"He's the one"

"What say thee, you point
Your thumb"
Runes are nice but your
Feelings are none
"Who will cramp first"
"You or my thumb"
She screams a laugh
With green eyed jealous
Passion.
She went red straight to
Him, He only wants one
Thing. And mines is not
Hers to sell

AZURE BONDS

Azure bonds the heavenly light
Don't breathe to fiercely you'll give it
A fright
Lovely beholding a cold winters day
Pretty lifelike of an ancient way
Is it a dragon's tail?
Or a peacock feather?
Will it pierce my soul with warmer
Weather?
Or chain me to the workman's
Tether?
Azure bonds you wondrous sight
Straight out of heaven with
Blue misty light
It's fading now I knew it wouldn't
Last
Those Azure bonds fade into the past

TRUE

Treasure stolen from the Ark
Treasure stolen in the dark
Place your lips on my heart
Maybe then you'll see the start
Of my love
For you I would lie so
Still
That only a giant from
A hill
Could move me away
From you
But you know such things
Aren't true

ROSE OF LOVE

Love washing over our souls
Life without hate or war are our
Goals
Try taking back some of that
Freedom they stole
With or without love we will
Find peace
So that we can set our
Minds at ease
Cease the rose of love if
You please
Slowly but surely she
Shows you her tease
In her bed you feel at ease
And you find her body so
Easy to please
Even tho' it's all a tease

LIES

Slowly walking towards the
Sun
Sharply talking to your loved
One
It's all in the eyes
Tearing through the disguise
To see through life's many lies
Is it radio or TV?
It's neither can't you see
Both lie and both seize
Many talk about the pains
Of life
But I'd rather sleep with your
Wife
Rather than feel the piercing
Of your eyes

DANCE ON

Dance on souls of love
For we have been blessed from
Above
We move gracefully for
A captive audience
The angels laugh and
Applaud us
I am the dragon with the
Golden heart
You are the light in my
Dark
We move forever to loves
Timeless beat
Ignoring the noise on the
Street

WOMAN SO DARK

The opening heart becomes so sweet
The feeling so strange we move to the
Beat Sugar and spice
That feeling so nice
A woman so dark
Yet not very old
The hold so stark
And turning cold
This feeling of love
Growing slightly old
And appearing from above

BITTER

It's quiet now with things
Silent
How can I live with this?
Silence

It's all for peace not even
The wind cries
The wars rage on with nothing
But bloodshed and hunger

But not here silent!
It speaks of peace
But gives of a chill
That leaves grave yards
Still

Yawning and crawling
Benzedrine pill
Whilst men of honour
Lie so still

The poppy wars
which the BNP sound
I think of their violence
I think of their crowds

I'd rather stay quiet
In this poor man's game
Ugly and violent
A yawning grave

You take up places
Whilst plastic comes
To Floyd like faces
If only it were true

An honourable death
But the sadness that comes
What have we done?

A world cries for a martyr
Whilst the Kingdom shows
Us
BITTER!!!!

MIDNIGHT BLUES (SONG)

How is the question
With time for a session
It's unbelievable this repression
So many go through it

I'm a sullen dancer
And midnight chance
An opium withdrawn
Glance

My words fumble with
A cannabis crumble
Got so much questioned
In my head, yes I wish I
Was dead

I'm a sullen dancer
And midnight chance
A Dragon poisoned
Glance

The hurt I have is so sharp
And clear I've looked at things
Through animalistic tears
Crying in this world

I'm a puppet dancing
And always chancing
Valium withdrawn glancing

Not so many angels in
My world leave it to me
I'll find a girl
All on an acid flashing swirl

I'm a sullen dancer
And a midnight chance
MIDNIGHT BLUES (SONG)

An opium withdrawn glance

Drugs go on the go in my
Hourglass which sands fall
So slow unknown to me
Are the numbers one and three

Valium withdrawn glancing
Opium withdrawn dancing
Dragon poised chancing
With all these things I'm
Bound to choose
The Valium
The Opium
Or the midnight blues
The Valium
The Opium
Or the midnight blues
The Valium
The Opium
Or the midnight blues

SUN

People tell you that love is for fools
They are the sad people who
Live their lives looking for something
They'll never find
Love is in happiness for the world
Love is in sharing feelings with
A boy or a girl
Love is a sun in a bright blue sky

TOMBS OF RUST

Dreams awakening to
Unhappy sleep
With games we are playing
Invisible creep
Slowly dawn comes,
With a smoke like sun
The moon was taken
And never returned
Love I've been forsaken
And left with excuses
The crown nearly mended
The friendliness overextended
Leaving it blended with
Tombs of rust
Tombs of rust, the bones
Put together
Poisons of pollution
A quiet insane grave
They think they have futures
Whilst the tombs of rust
Tombs of rust Yawning
On a drug addicts grave
A slave of passion it's
Always the same
Money, Diamonds a cocaine

Addicts trust
Sometimes it leads them
There to the Tombs of rust
Tombs of rust open
For the poppy slaves game
Some are misspoken
Some are Insane
So watch for the warnings
The heart attack may come
And left in warning
Are the Tombs of Rust
Tombs of Rust!!!

FORGOTTEN SUNS

Forgotten races
Under forgotten suns
They are the forgotten people
Who come
To me for advice
And to entice
Me to their world
I would gladly go
If it weren't for a girl

TOY

Let your tears go
We all know
That life can be painful and slow
It's so like love
Yet it's no show
It's like a fetish for gloves
When it's cold and icy as snow
Take your time
Feel some joy
Life is dark sometimes
Or life can be broken like a toy

AFTERWORD

THE BOOK IS PURELY FOR YOUR ATTENTION AND SHOULD BE TREATED WITH HOPE AND DIGNITY. LOVE YOU DAWN NO MATTER WHAT!!!!

www.ingramcontent.com/pod-product-compliance
Lightning Source LLC
Chambersburg PA
CBHW031412040426
42444CB00005B/532